DREAM JOBS IN MATH

COLIN HYNSON

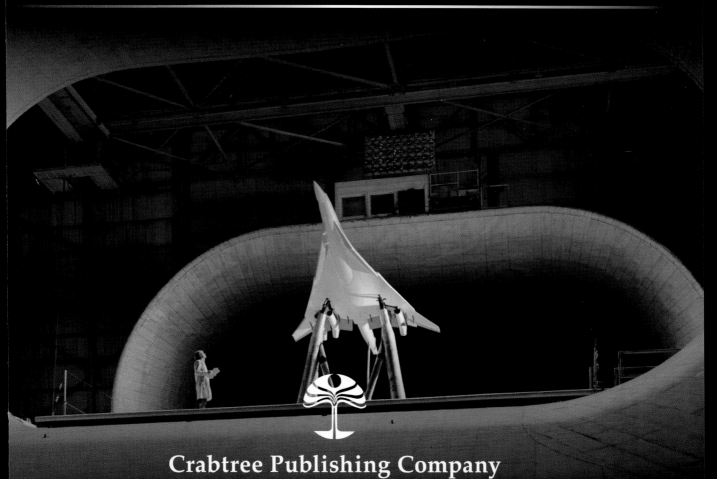

Crabtree Publishing Company

Crabtree Publishing Company
www.crabtreebooks.com
1-800-387-7650

Published in Canada
616 Welland Ave.
St. Catharines, ON
L2M 5V6

Published in the United States
PMB 59051
350 Fifth Ave. 59th Floor
New York, NY 10118

Published in 2017 by CRABTREE PUBLISHING COMPANY

First published in 2016 by Wayland
(A division of Hachette Children's Books)
Copyright © Wayland 2016

Author:
Colin Hynson

Editors:
Victoria Brooker
Jon Richards
Petrice Custance

Designer:
Darren Jordan

Proofreader:
Wendy Scavuzzo

Print and production coordinator:
Katherine Berti

Photo credits
1, 26–27 courtesy of NASA, 2, 12–13 Dreamstime.com/Jevtic, 3, 10–11 Clauddiusmm, 4b Dreamstime.com/Alexandr Sandvoss, 5cr Dreamstime.com/Juraj Lipták, 5b courtesy of NASA, 6–7 courtesy of NSA, 7tr Dreamstime.com/Antares614, 8–9 Dreamstime.com/Stephen Griffith, 9tr Wylve creative commons attribution, 11br Dreamstime.com/Benkrut, 13cl Dreamstime.com/Motorolka, 14–15 Dreamstime.com/Badoff, 15tr Puramyun31 creative commons attribution, 16bl Dreamstime.com/Zhukovsky, 16–17 Dreamstime.com/Kenneth D Durden, 17tr Dreamstime.com/Zhukovsky, 18bl courtesy of NOAA, 18–19 Dreamstime.com/Skolton, 19tl Dreamstime.com/Nataliavo, 20bl Sean Devine creative commons attribution, 20–21 Dreamstime.com/Rfischia, 21tr Maximilian Schönherr creative commons attribution, 22bl Dreamstime.com/Moreno Soppelsa, 23br, 31br Dreamstime.com/Aniram, 24–25 Dreamstime.com/Pablo Hidalgo, 25tr Palosirkka, 25bl Dreamstime.com/Gillespaire, 26bl courtesy of NASA, 27br courtesy of SpaceX, 28bl Dreamstime.com/Prykhodov, 28–29 Dreamstime.com/Andriy Rovenko

Library and Archives Canada Cataloguing in Publication

Hynson, Colin, author
    Dream jobs in math / Colin Hynson.

(Cutting-edge careers in STEM)
Issued in print and electronic formats.
ISBN 978-0-7787-2963-1 (hardback).--
ISBN 978-0-7787-2971-6 (paperback).--
ISBN 978-1-4271-1861-5 (html)

    1. Mathematics--Vocational guidance--Juvenile literature.
I. Title.

QA10.5.H96 2016   j510.23   C2016-906638-X
                                          C2016-906639-8

Library of Congress Cataloging-in-Publication Data
Names: Hynson, Colin.
Title: Dream jobs in math / Colin Hynson.
Description: New York, N.Y. : Crabtree Publishing Company, 2017. | Series: Cutting-edge careers in STEM | Audience: Age 10-14. | Audience: Grade 7 to 8. | Includes index.
Identifiers: LCCN 2016045933 (print) | LCCN 2016046744 (ebook) | ISBN 9780778729631 (hardcover : alk. paper) | ISBN 9780778729716 (pbk. : alk. paper) | ISBN 9781427118615 (Electronic book text)
Subjects: LCSH: Mathematics--Vocational guidance--Juvenile literature.
Classification: LCC QA10.5 .H94 2017 (print) | LCC QA10.5 (ebook) | DDC 510.23--dc23
LC record available at https://lccn.loc.gov/2016045933

Printed in Hong Kong/012017/BK20161024

CONTENTS

MATH

JOBS IN MATH

QUALIFICATIONS IN MATH CAN TAKE YOU FROM HI-TECH MOTOR RACING TO THE EXCITING REALM OF MOVIE MAKING!

Welcome to the world of working in mathematics. Studying math is really worthwhile, because it opens doors to a whole range of interesting, exciting, unusual, and amazing jobs in mathematics. Studying math doesn't mean you'll be stuck in a lecture hall or classroom. There are also jobs in code breaking, food production, and disaster relief, to name a few. This book will help you find out what each job is all about, as well as the rewards of doing the job.

▶ Formula One designers use high-end math skills to work out how air will flow over their cars.

STEM STANDS FOR **S**CIENCE, **T**ECHNOLOGY, **E**NGINEERING, AND **M**ATH. AS SCIENCE, TECHNOLOGY, AND ENGINEERING INDUSTRIES GROW, THERE IS INCREASING DEMAND FOR PEOPLE WITH STEM SKILLS.

▼ An education in science could take you to one of the most prestigious colleges or universities on the planet, such as Oxford University or MIT.

THE ROUTE TO

SECONDARY SCHOOL:
Education from about ages 14 to 18

A MATH JOB

POST-SECONDARY: Studying for an **undergraduate degree** and a post-graduate degree, such as a **master's degree** and a **doctorate**

5

SUBJECTS AND QUALIFICATIONS

For each job, you will find out what subjects you may study as you move through school, and what further training you would need. These are quite general because what you study for a particular qualification will change depending on which country you are in.

▼ Predicting powerful **hurricanes** requires some incredible number crunching.

CRACKING CODES

KEEPING OUR VITAL DATA SAFE IS BECOMING A VERY IMPORTANT JOB.

6

Cryptology uses math codes to make sure any information that is shared **online** can only be read by those who have the key to that code. This is called **encryption**. The job of the cryptologist is to make sure that our information is protected from people who are trying to find our personal details to use for illegal activities. These can include identity theft, taking money from bank accounts, or making telephone calls using someone else's number. Cryptologists create codes that are meant to be impossible to break, but they are also involved in trying to crack other people's codes.

▶ The US National Security Agency (NSA) has its headquarters at Fort Meade, Maryland.

CRYPTOLOGISTS ALSO WORK FOR THE SECURITY SERVICES TRYING TO LISTEN IN TO THE MESSAGES OF CRIMINALS. TO DO THIS, IT'S ALSO HELPFUL TO SPEAK AT LEAST ONE FOREIGN LANGUAGE, AS MESSAGES COULD COME FROM ANYWHERE IN THE WORLD.

WHAT YOU DO

As a cryptologist, much of your work will be office-based. You will use your math skills to create new codes and test those codes to make sure that they cannot be broken. You will also go back to any codes being used to make sure that they are still reliable. Because security is so important to companies and governments, you will be an important member of a team protecting all their valuable information.

▶ Banks use coded card readers to protect people's account details.

7

WHERE YOU WORK

The number of opportunities for cryptologists is growing all the time as more and more of our lives move online. You'll find work with banks, computer companies, and other businesses both large and small. Many cryptologists are employed by the police, military, and security services, such as NSA in the US and the Canadian Security Intelligence Service (CSIS) in Canada.

THE ROUTE TO CRYPTOLOGY

YOU MAY NEED TO STUDY:

SECONDARY SCHOOL:
Computer science and math

POST-SECONDARY: Math or computer science.
Some universities offer degrees in cryptology.

DURING WORLD WAR II, THE GERMANS USED A MACHINE CALLED ENIGMA THAT COULD CODE MESSAGES WITH A POSSIBLE 159 QUINTILLION COMBINATIONS. THAT'S 159 FOLLOWED BY 18 ZEROS!

TRANSIT PLANNING

8

TOP MATH SKILLS ARE NEEDED TO GET PEOPLE FROM POINT A TO B AS EFFICIENTLY AS POSSIBLE.

Transportation planners improve and manage road, rail, and airport routes. Whenever a new building project is started, transportation planners are involved right from the start. They have to make sure that the new homes, offices, or stores being built are easy to reach, and that they do not create any transportation problems in the surrounding area. By getting the design right, we'll all be able to travel quickly, safely, and in a way that protects the environment.

THERE ARE MORE THAN 250 MILLION CARS AND TRUCKS IN THE UNITED STATES ALONE.

WHAT YOU DO

As a transportation planner, you will spend a lot of your time examining **statistics**. These will help you predict what will happen when a new road, railway line, or airport is built. You will be working as part of a team that might include urban planners, architects, and people concerned about the environment. You might also be involved in meeting members of the public and asking them what transportation improvements they would like to see in their area.

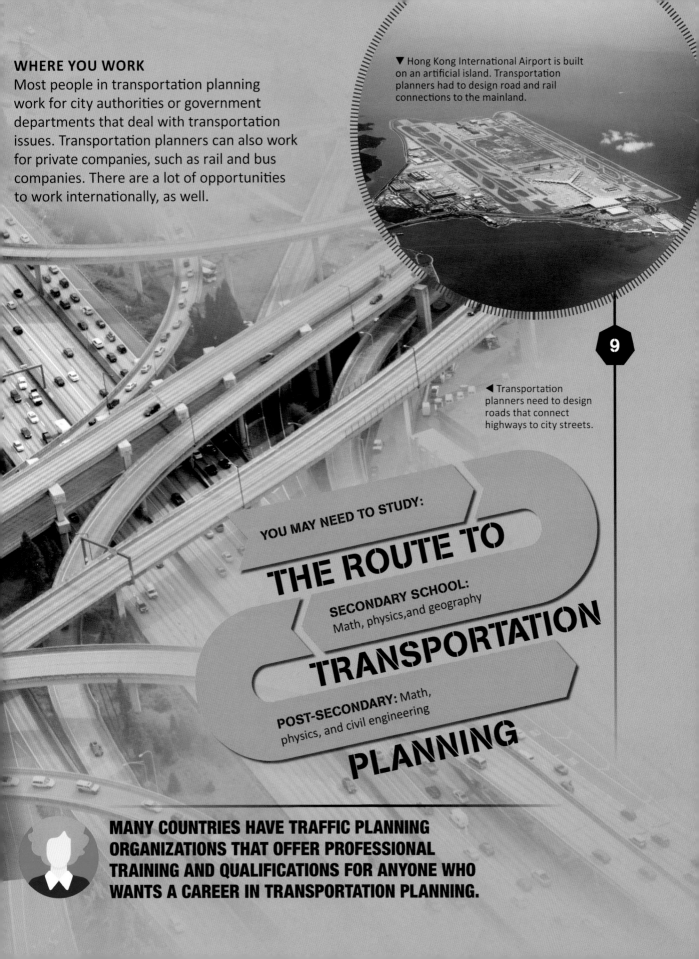

WHERE YOU WORK

Most people in transportation planning work for city authorities or government departments that deal with transportation issues. Transportation planners can also work for private companies, such as rail and bus companies. There are a lot of opportunities to work internationally, as well.

▼ Hong Kong International Airport is built on an artificial island. Transportation planners had to design road and rail connections to the mainland.

◄ Transportation planners need to design roads that connect highways to city streets.

YOU MAY NEED TO STUDY:

THE ROUTE TO

SECONDARY SCHOOL:
Math, physics, and geography

TRANSPORTATION

POST-SECONDARY: Math, physics, and civil engineering

PLANNING

MANY COUNTRIES HAVE TRAFFIC PLANNING ORGANIZATIONS THAT OFFER PROFESSIONAL TRAINING AND QUALIFICATIONS FOR ANYONE WHO WANTS A CAREER IN TRANSPORTATION PLANNING.

MAPPING THE PLANET

CARTOGRAPHERS MAKE SENSE OF A WHOLE WORLD OF INFORMATION.

You might think that the world has been well mapped by now. But the landscape around us is constantly changing and the need for new maps is growing all the time. Cartographers are called upon to create all kinds of specialized maps. A cartographer has to gather this information, sometimes from satellites in orbit, and convert it into a form that is useful.

YOU MAY NEED TO STUDY:

THE ROUTE TO

SECONDARY SCHOOL: Math, science, geography, and computer sciences

CARTOGRAPHY

POST-SECONDARY: There are some universities that offer degrees in Geographic Information Systems, but a degree in math, geography, or Earth sciences is also useful.

ONE OF THE FASTEST-GROWING AREAS OF MAP-MAKING IS CALLED GEOVISUALIZATION. **THIS INVOLVES THE CREATION OF INTERACTIVE AND ANIMATED MAPS THAT CAN DISPLAY VAST AMOUNTS OF INFORMATION AND CAN BE CONSTANTLY UPDATED.**

WHERE YOU WORK

All sorts of businesses need people with cartographic skills. You could work for companies that specialize in oil and gas exploration. Building companies and suppliers of gas, electricity, and water also have to have accurate and up-to-date maps. There are also many publishers who print maps and travel guides for the tourist and travel industry. Governments and local authorities also need cartographers to assist in the planning of new roads, homes, hospitals, and schools.

IT IS ESTIMATED THAT THERE ARE MORE THAN 2,500 SATELLITES IN ORBIT AROUND EARTH.

11

◀ This cartographer is equipped to collect information out in the field, with a laser **range finder**, a **GPS** receiver, and a rugged computer.

WHAT YOU DO

The working day of a cartographer can be divided into two main parts. The first is to collect and analyze the data that is needed to create a map. If you are working on a particular project, part of this work is to decide what information is useful and what can be ignored. Once you have gathered all the information you need, you will start designing the map. You will have to design the map so that it can be useful any way it is seen.

▶ A cartographer sets up a GPS receiver to collect data.

FEEDING THE WORLD

BIOSTATISTICS HELP FARMERS AND FOOD COMPANIES FEED THE WORLD.

Biologists create a lot of data in their work. This needs to be analyzed and presented so that they can understand their own work. Biostatisticians will be part of a team that will grow "trial" crops using a new seed. They will watch the crop grow and see how it compares to other crops. Biostatistics are also used in the field of medicine and drug research to test drugs before they are offered to doctors.

THE ROUTE TO

YOU MAY NEED TO STUDY:

SECONDARY SCHOOL:
Math, biology, and computer science

POST-SECONDARY: There are some universities that offer degrees in biostatistics or biomathematics, and a degree in math is also a good route.

BIOSTATISTICS

A FEW BIOSTATISTICIANS WORK WITH HEALTH CHARITIES, STUDYING TO SEE HOW MANY PEOPLE ARE SUFFERING FROM MALNUTRITION OR HAVE DISEASES LINKED TO A POOR DIET OR A LACK OF CLEAN WATER.

▼ Plants are studied in the laboratory as well as the field.

WHERE YOU WORK

The two main areas of work for biostatisticians are in agriculture and in medicine. There are agricultural companies that specialize in creating new kinds of seeds for farmers or manufacture fertilizers and insecticides. Medical companies produce new drugs and other treatments for people who are sick. Government agencies that create the rules that agricultural and medical companies have to follow, also employ biostatisticians to examine information given to them by those companies.

13

◀ Data is collected by studying how well new crops grow.

WHAT YOU DO

As a biostatistician, much of your day will be spent either in the laboratory or in the office. You will usually be working as part of a team with other scientists. Some of your working day will require communication with others either face-to-face, on the phone, or by email.

THE BIGGER PICTURE

▼ Collecting huge amounts of data requires large **server farms**, such as these banks of computers.

BIG DATA **ANALYSTS STUDY MASSES OF INFORMATION TO SPOT THE LATEST TRENDS.**

These analysts are trying to predict what people might want in the future. For Big Data Analysts this is called "predictive analysis." They have to examine the data to see if they can identify any hidden **trends** that will continue into the future. This could include what products are selling in a store, or even how government services are being used by members of the public.

WHAT YOU DO

Most of your working day will be spent in the office collecting and analyzing data. There are plenty of opportunities to travel to other locations so that you can collect that data. You will also have to spend some of your time presenting your analysis to the organization you are working for. This will mean that you will have to be able to show your findings in a way that they can understand.

EVERY DAY, THE AMOUNT OF DATA CREATED AROUND THE WORLD COULD FILL THE HARD DRIVES OF 2.5 MILLION DESKTOP COMPUTERS.

THE "INTERNET OF THINGS" IS A SYSTEM OF EVERYDAY OBJECTS FROM MACHINES IN A FACTORY TO DEVICES YOU WEAR, WHICH HAVE BUILT-IN SENSORS THAT GATHER AND TRANSFER DATA. THIS INFORMATION CAN TELL PEOPLE ALL SORTS OF THINGS, FROM WHAT EXERCISE IS POPULAR TO WHETHER YOU NEED TO BUY MORE MILK.

▲ This fridge is connected to the Internet and can order more food when supplies run low.

YOU MAY NEED TO STUDY:

SECONDARY SCHOOL:
Math and computer science

THE ROUTE TO

POST-SECONDARY: Math, business studies, marketing, or computer science

BIG DATA ANALYSIS

WHERE YOU WORK

The demand for Big Data Analysts is growing all the time. Most Big Data Analysts work in the areas of finance, such as banks, stores, and online buying and selling. Other Big Data Analysts work for market research companies. Market research companies specialize in gathering and analyzing information for organizations that cannot do it themselves.

SPORTS STATISTICS

MATH CAN IMPROVE AN ATHLETE'S PERFORMANCE AND TAKE THEM TO VICTORY.

The first duty of a sports statistician is to gather information on sports performances. This is usually done while the game is being played, by taking notes on how well an athlete is doing or by looking at the performance of the team as a whole. Before the game, a statistician can also analyze information about the opposing team to look for weaknesses and where they might be dangerous.

DISTANCE RUN BY ATHLETES DURING ONE GAME:
BASEBALL – 0.046 MILES (0.074 KM)
FOOTBALL – 1.2 MILES (2 KM)
BASKETBALL – 2.9 MILES (4.6 KM)
TENNIS – 3 MILES (4.8 KM)
SOCCER – 7 MILES (11.2 KM)

▼ A football team may use a statistician to spot any weaknesses in their own style of play.

▼ Sports statisticians work with individual athletes and suggest improvements during training and during a game.

WHAT YOU DO

Most sporting events happen either on weekends or in the evening, and you will be expected to be there. Of course, if you love the sport that you're working in, this will be a bonus. During the rest of the week, you will spend your time analyzing the information that you have gathered, and presenting that information in a way that is useful for team managers, players, and television commentators.

WHERE YOU WORK

Many of the big sports teams employ their own sports statisticians. You will need to build expertise in both the sport and the team that's playing it. There are also some businesses that specialize in providing sports statistics. Smaller teams or other sports agencies use these specialized businesses if they do not have their own statistician. Sports statisticians also work for television companies, websites, and newspapers that supply sports commentaries.

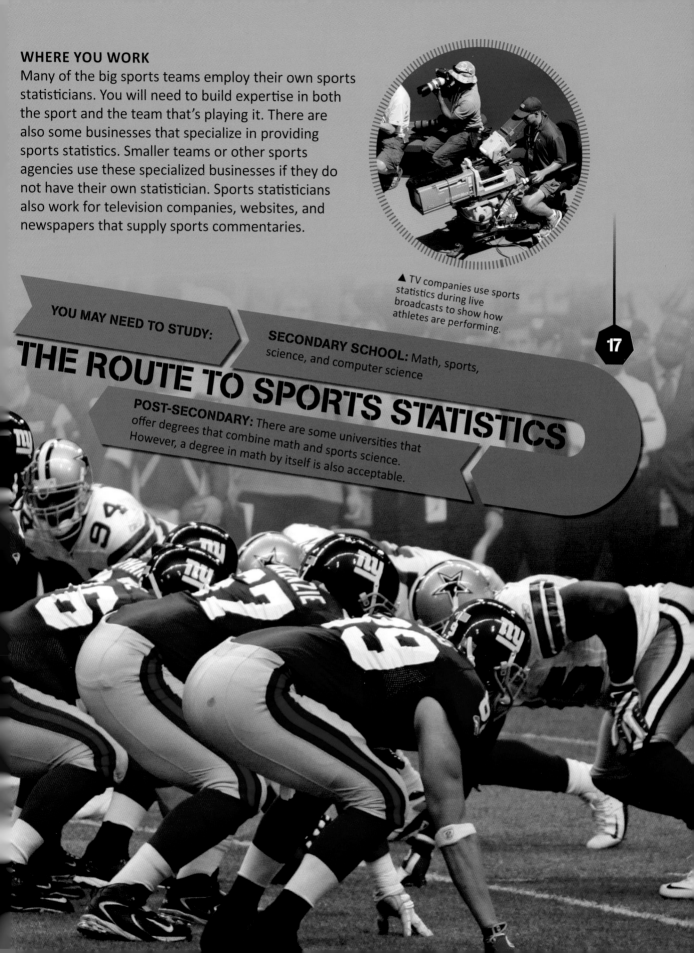

▲ TV companies use sports statistics during live broadcasts to show how athletes are performing.

YOU MAY NEED TO STUDY:

THE ROUTE TO SPORTS STATISTICS

SECONDARY SCHOOL: Math, sports, science, and computer science

POST-SECONDARY: There are some universities that offer degrees that combine math and sports science. However, a degree in math by itself is also acceptable.

SHAPING OUR CLIMATE

MATH CAN PREDICT THE WEATHER AND CREATE MODELS OF HOW IT WILL ACT.

People working in the field of climate modeling collect data about changes in weather patterns over a long period of time. This information includes the level of rainfall, temperatures, the amount of ice at the poles, and the frequency of extreme weather events such as hurricanes, floods, and tornadoes. Climate modelers can then build a mathematical picture of the **climate** today and see how it has changed. Using this information, they can then predict what will happen in the future.

▼ Climate modelers try to predict how often extreme events, such as flooding, may occur.

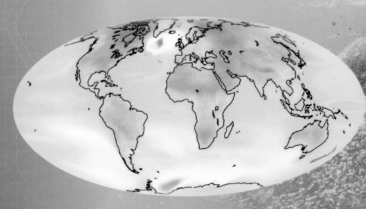

▲ Climate modelers create maps of how conditions may change, such as this one which shows how temperatures will get warmer up to the year 2050.

WHAT YOU DO

Climate modelers usually spend most of their working hours analyzing data and creating models. However, you will have to spend some of your time finding ways to present your findings that are easy to understand. There are also opportunities to visit weather stations and weather ships to help with the gathering of information on weather changes.

▲ Small stations collect information about the weather.

YOU MAY NEED TO STUDY:

THE ROUTE TO

SECONDARY SCHOOL:
Math, science (especially physics and chemistry), and geography

CLIMATE MODELING

POST-SECONDARY: Earth science, **meteorology** (the science of weather), or environmental science

WHERE YOU WORK

Most climate modelers work for universities or national or international agencies, such as the World Meteorological Organization. There are also some businesses that specialize in providing climate models for other businesses. For example, an energy company might want information on changes in climate in a particular area before deciding to build wind turbines or solar panels.

CLIMATE MODELING CAN BE USED BY AGRICULTURAL INDUSTRIES. DATA CAN SHOW HOW CHANGES IN CONDITIONS MIGHT AFFECT CROPS GROWN IN AREAS, OR SHOW WHICH CROPS COULD BE GROWN INSTEAD.

VISUAL EFFECTS

MANY MOVIES USE MATH POWER TO ADD DRAMA AND EXCITEMENT.

Visual effects (or VFX) programmers are the people who create the computerized special effects in a movie. This is often called **CGI** (Computer–Generated Imagery). People who work in VFX programming need strong math skills, especially in geometry, as well as computer programming, and have artistic abilities.

▼ Actors are filmed against a blue screen and effects are added afterward.

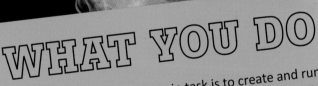

WHAT YOU DO

A VFX programmer's main task is to create and run computer programs, which are then used to create a particular special effect. This could be anything, such as a fleet of spacecraft flying across the night sky, a huge monster climbing a mountain, or a lightning storm over a desert. Many of these special effects could be created without the use of computers, but they would not look realistic enough or may simply take too long to create.

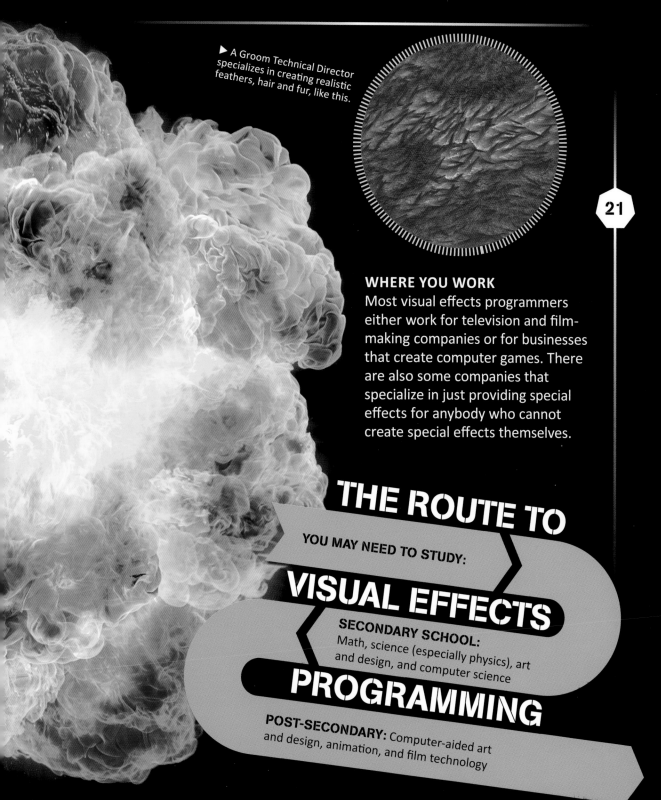

 SOME VFX PROGRAMMERS BECOME SPECIALISTS IN ONE PARTICULAR AREA. THERE ARE PROGRAMMERS WHOSE ONLY JOBS ARE TO CREATE REALISTIC SKY AND CLOUDS OR TO CREATE REALISTIC EXPLOSIONS.

▶ A Groom Technical Director specializes in creating realistic feathers, hair and fur, like this.

21

WHERE YOU WORK

Most visual effects programmers either work for television and film-making companies or for businesses that create computer games. There are also some companies that specialize in just providing special effects for anybody who cannot create special effects themselves.

THE ROUTE TO

YOU MAY NEED TO STUDY:

VISUAL EFFECTS

SECONDARY SCHOOL:
Math, science (especially physics), art and design, and computer science

PROGRAMMING

POST-SECONDARY: Computer-aided art and design, animation, and film technology

DIGITAL FORENSICS

THE JOB OF A DIGITAL FORENSICS EXPERT IS BECOMING MORE AND MORE CENTRAL TO POLICE INVESTIGATIONS.

22

Police forces use **forensics** scientists to help solve crimes. Digital forensics experts look for **evidence** on any digital device, such as a computer or a cell phone. Many people do not realize that whenever they use a digital device like a computer or cell phone they are leaving a trail. If somebody makes a call on a cell phone, this trail will include who they called, what time the call was made, where the caller was at the time, and how long the call lasted. This evidence will still exist, even if the caller deletes it from their phone. An expert can retrieve this data and submit it as evidence.

◀ This equipment is being used to recover data from a computer hard drive.

WHAT YOU DO

Although you will spend time searching for evidence on digital devices, you will also have to make sure that the evidence you have gathered is easy to understand and can be used in court. This will mean that there will be times when you will have to work evenings and weekends to help the police. You may also have to appear in court as an **expert witness** and help find evidence at the scene of a crime.

ONE OF THE MOST COMPLICATED AREAS FOR DIGITAL FORENSICS EXPERTS IS THE AREA OF FINANCIAL CRIME, SUCH AS TAX EVASION, FORGERY, OR HACKING INTO A BANK ACCOUNT.

YOU MAY NEED TO STUDY:

THE ROUTE TO

SECONDARY SCHOOL:
Math, science, and computer science

DIGITAL FORENSICS

POST-SECONDARY: Computer science

▼ Digital criminals can be very good at hiding evidence, so a digital forensics expert has to be better!

WHERE YOU WORK

Most digital forensics experts work for police forces. They are brought into an investigation because of their skills in finding data on digital devices. International policing organizations, such as INTERPOL, EUROPOL, and the United Nations police, also employ digital forensics experts when they are trying to solve crimes that cross national borders.

Some estimates say that cybercrime causes nearly $500 billion of damage to the global economy every year.

******

DEALING WITH DISASTER

THIS MATH JOB MAKES SURE THAT RESOURCES GET TO WHERE THEY ARE NEEDED.

The job of a humanitarian logistician is making sure that the right supplies get to the right place in the aftermath of a disaster. This task starts well before disaster strikes. Humanitarian logisticians see what sort of disasters might strike a region. They also collect data such as population sizes and what hospitals are available. When a disaster does occur, they are then involved in distributing **aid** and helping the people recover in the short- and long-term.

YOU MAY NEED TO STUDY:

THE ROUTE TO AID LOGISTICS

SECONDARY SCHOOL: Math, science, and geography

POST-SECONDARY: There are some universities that offer degrees in **logistics**. Studying math, business studies, or management will also be useful.

WHERE YOU WORK

Most humanitarian logisticians will work for charities that deal with disaster relief. Organizations such as Oxfam, the Red Cross, and the Red Crescent are all involved in preparing for disasters and acting when disaster strikes. There will also be opportunities to work in different parts of the world.

◀ Aid workers hand out supplies in the aftermath of an earthquake in Ecuador.

▼ Long-term help includes repairing water supplies and drilling wells.

WHAT YOU DO

As a humanitarian logistician, you will spend some of your time doing office-based work using data to plan for disasters. You will also travel to places where supplies are being stored to see that they are ready to use at any time. If a disaster does strike, you may have to travel to the affected region to make sure supplies are arriving safely and being distributed in the right way.

FARTHER AND FASTER

▼ An engineer checks the model of an experimental aircraft before testing in a giant **wind tunnel**.

THIS MATH JOB PUSHES VEHICLES TO THE VERY LIMIT AND BEYOND.

An aerodynamicist studies how air flows around a car or an aircraft, and how that affects its performance. They will try to find ways of making that vehicle move faster, travel farther, or be more economical. It's not just the shape of the vehicle that aerodynamicists work on. They will also be involved in the design of any electrical parts on the vehicle, the fuel system that is being used, and the choice of material for building all or part of the vehicle. **Aerodynamics** is important in all of these areas.

▼ This computer model shows how air flows over the wing of an experimental aircraft.

WHAT YOU DO

Aerodynamicists create 3-D computer models of the vehicles they are designing. They will also spend some of their time building real models of vehicles that will then be tested in wind tunnels. Wind tunnels show how air flows around vehicles when they are moving. Once that part of the test is over, the vehicle will have to be tested outside of the laboratory. This means that you will spend some of your time outdoors gathering data on the tests.

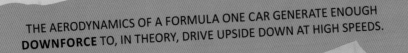

THE AERODYNAMICS OF A FORMULA ONE CAR GENERATE ENOUGH DOWNFORCE TO, IN THEORY, DRIVE UPSIDE DOWN AT HIGH SPEEDS.

YOU MAY NEED TO STUDY:

SECONDARY SCHOOL: Math, science (especially physics), art and design, and engineering

THE ROUTE TO AERODYNAMICS

POST-SECONDARY: Some universities offer degrees in aerodynamic engineering, but studying engineering is also a good entry to working in aerodynamics.

▶ Some private companies, such as SpaceX, are now involved in designing spacecraft.

WHERE YOU WORK

Aerodynamicists work for companies that design and build vehicles, including cars, aircraft, and even spacecraft. You could be working on new vehicles or improving existing vehicles. Some aerodynamicists work for government transportation departments, making sure that vehicles meet any rules and regulations about safety and pollution levels.

THE NEXT BIG THING

RECORDING COMPANIES GO TO GREAT LENGTHS TO FIND THE NEXT HIT BAND.

The music industry produces a huge amount of data. This comes from music sales, both online **downloads** and physical purchases, and through **streaming** services. Music data analysts can use this data to see which bands are popular in which parts of the world. Record companies can then use this information to promote acts.

◄ Streaming now accounts for about 30 percent of digital music revenues.

WHAT YOU DO

Much of your working day as a music d[...] analyst will be gathering and analyzing d[...] from online music sites. This will also inclu[...] **social media** websites so you can spot [...] bands that are just starting to build u[...] following. You will have to work with o[...] people who work in other parts of the m[...] industry, such as marketing and promoti[...]

THE ILLEGAL COPYING OF MUSIC HAS BEEN A BIG PROBLEM FOR MUSICIANS AND RECORD COMPANIES. MUSIC DATA ANALYSTS CAN HELP TO SHUT DOWN ANY PIRACY SITES THEY FIND DURING THEIR RESEARCH.

▼ As an analyst, you might also have to go to live performances to monitor which bands and even which songs are becoming popular. You might spot the next Cold Play!

WHERE YOU WORK
Music data analysts usually work for record labels who sign up musicians and release their music for people to listen to. Music streaming services, such as Spotify or Deezer, also employ music data analysts to research how people are using them.

YOU MAY NEED TO STUDY:

SECONDARY SCHOOL:
Math, computer science, and music

THE ROUTE TO

POST-SECONDARY: Music, math, or computer science

MUSIC DATA ANALYSIS

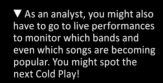

GLOSSARY

AERODYNAMICS
The study of the way air moves around solid objects

AID
Support and help that is sent to an area that has suffered a disaster; Aid can take the form of people who can supply services, such as rescue workers and doctors, or as food, clothing, and shelter.

BIG DATA
Huge amounts of data that is collected and stored on computers; Studying this data can reveal large-scale trends and insights into how people are behaving.

BIOSTATISTICS
Using statistics and data to study biological activity, such as how crops grow and how medicines perform

CGI
Short for Computer-Generated Imagery. It refers to images and effects that are created digitally on a computer and applied to a movie or TV program once filming has finished.

CLIMATE
The average pattern of weather in one place over a period of 30 years

CRYPTOLOGY
The study of codes and the devices used to create them

DEGREE
The qualification given by universities after a period of study—normally three to four years

DOCTORATE
One of the highest education qualifications students can achieve

DOWNFORCE
A downward force created by air passing over a vehicle; Fast cars use downforce to push them down into the road to improve their handling.

DOWNLOADS
Digital files that are copied off the Internet and onto a computer

ENCRYPTION
Converting data into a code that cannot be read by anyone except the people with the key to the code

EVIDENCE
Physical or verbal information that can be produced to prove a person's guilt during a criminal trial

EXPERT WITNESS
A person who is specialized in a particular subject and gives his or her expert opinion in a court

FORENSICS
Using scientific and mathematical techniques to help solve crimes

GEOVISUALIZATION
Turning data into maps and charts

GPS
GPS stands for Global Positioning System; There's a network of 24 satellites that send information and mapping data to GPS receivers.

HURRICANES
Huge tropical storms that form over an ocean

LOGISTICS
Organizing and controlling the movement of things from one place to another

MASTER'S DEGREE
A qualification given by universities; It is normally given after a degree and before a doctorate.

METEOROLOGY
The study of the weather and how it is created by events in Earth's atmosphere

ONLINE
Something that is found on the Internet

PIRACY
Using or taking something without the owner's permission; On the Internet, this can include posting and sharing films and music.

RANGE FINDER
A device that calculates the distance from one object to another

SERVER FARM
A cluster of computers that is able to store vast amounts of data

SOCIAL MEDIA
Websites and software that allow people to communicate with each other socially

STATISTICS
A branch of mathematics that collects and examines numbers

STREAMING
Listening to music or watching a video that is sent as a continuous stream of data across the Internet

TRENDS
Behavior that has become a fashion and is being carried out by increasing numbers of people

UNDERGRADUATE
A person who is studying at a university for their first degree

WIND TUNNEL
A building or room where wind can be produced artificially; Wind tunnels are used to test the aerodynamics of vehicles.

INDEX